Stringed Instruments

By Debbie Croft

T0342747

Contents

Stringed Instruments in an Orchestra

There are four types of stringed instruments that make up the string section in an orchestra. They are the violin, the viola, the cello and the double bass.

violin and viola

cello

double bass

cellist Yo-Yo Ma

Each of these instruments has four tuned strings and a hollow body made of wood. Sound vibrates inside the body of the instrument when the bow is drawn across the strings.

The strings on the instrument are made of nylon, steel or gut, and extend along the body and neck. They are secured to small pegs that are individually tightened or loosened to tune each string. The handle of the bow is made of wood, and the strings are real horsehair.

The violin is the smallest in size and has the highest pitch of the four instruments. One end of the violin rests under the violinist's chin. The neck of the instrument is supported with one hand. The fingers of this hand are placed in different positions along the strings. This changes the pitch of the notes when the bow is drawn across the strings.

The viola is very similar in appearance to the violin, except that it is larger and therefore produces a deeper sound. It is also played with a bow, in a similar way to the violin.

Next in increasing size is the cello. Because of its larger size, the cellist sits on a chair and straddles the instrument while its base rests on the floor. Again, the bow is drawn across the strings to produce notes of varying pitch.

The double bass is the largest stringed instrument. The bassist stands behind the instrument, which rests on the floor. The double bass has the lowest sound of all the stringed instruments. It can be played with a bow, or by plucking the strings to create a different sound.

Although each of these instruments has a unique sound, they are often played together in an orchestra to create a harmonious blend of musical notes.

The String Recital

Venue: School Hall   Date: 4 March

Instrument: Strings

ADJUDICATOR'S REPORT

It gives me great pleasure to judge the string recital today. Each performance highlighted the hard work of these gifted musicians. The standard of the music we enjoyed is proof of the hours of practice put in by the competitors and they should all be congratulated for doing their best.

In particular, I would like to focus on the performance of Lucy. For such a young performer, she played the violin brilliantly. I am envious of her musical ability!

Lucy's presentation was complete in every respect. Her movement on and off the stage, her placement of the violin and her choice of music were excellent. These factors combined to provide us with a performance worthy of high praise.

Lucy's nimble finger work in the quaver passage would usually be associated with someone who has been playing for many years. To have developed this skill by the age of twelve is quite remarkable. The expression in Lucy's performance and her attention to detail created a very pure sound.

If you have ever tried to play the violin, you would realise how much effort is required to play like this. I'm sure Lucy has practised that piece many times. She has had to memorise the notes and learn the difficult parts that no doubt caused some problems in the early stages.

This performance deserves to be heard by more people than just those who are here today. It should be presented as a model for all the other musicians who strive to achieve excellence. One would have to travel a long way to find a more moving and polished performance.

Congratulations, everyone. Today you have shared with us the magic of your talent, and for that we feel extremely fortunate. Thank you for the privilege of hearing your music.

Adjudicator: .... *Jane Stewart* ....